STILL NO KIDS & STILL OK

ELLEN METTER

Browser Press
Denver, Colorado

For the children
I chose not to
conceive. You're most
welcome!

Still No Kids & Still Ok

Text and illustrations by Ellen Metter

Cover photo from PickPik.

Cartoon credits:
Nuclear Button baby derived and licensed from arlatis - vector 3589141.
Tuition Increase prone figure derived from Vectortoons image.
I'm Ok cartoon includes window casement image ID 131938654 by Zdenek Sasek licensed from Dreamstime.com.

Copyright © 2024 Ellen Metter. All Rights Reserved.

Cataloging-in-Publication Data
Metter, Ellen.
      Still No Kids & Still Ok : A childfree humor book / by Ellen Metter.
118pp. : ill.
ISBN 978-0-9711627-1-6
1. Childfree – Humor. I.Title.
HQ755
306.87

Contents

Why this Book?
- We've Come a Long Way, Baby! / 9
- Cheerfully Choosing / 10

1. Why Be Childfree? / 11
- Mama Me? Oy! / 12
- Choosing the Right Curtain / 17
- A Little Help from Myself / 24
- I Only Wanna Be with Me / 27
- Money Can't Buy Me Kids / 32
- All Your Fault! / 34
- Ask Me if I Care? / 37
- Multiply Something Else / 39
- Who You Calling Selfish? / 41
- Ain't Nobody's Business but My Own / 45

2. Conception is Still a Thing / 48
- How Do They Do It? / 54
- It's True That Kids are Essential / 56
- Give the Kid a Break, but Not a Frosé / 60
- It's Gonna Be Great! / 63
- Like Father Like Son? / 63
- Population Implosion / 65
- Is it Worth the Effort? / 67
- It Just Ain't Easy / 70

- Teens Can be Handy / 72
- Yes, I'm Still Sure / 74
- Your Kids May Have Kids / 76
- Give Us a Break / 77
- Conception is Still a Thing / 79

3. **Over-60, Childfree, & Still Ok? / 80**
    - My Cuteness Epiphany / 80
    - The Young'uns Have Their Charms / 86
    - No Kids, No Problems? / 87
- Annoying Assumptions / 92
- My Friends Kids / 94
- Tiny But Tidy / 99
- The Parents Gang / 101
- Still Crazy After All These Years? / 103
- Who Loves Ya, Baby? / 105
- No Perfect Choice / 108
- Poor Old Childfree Me / 111
- You're Welcome / 114

Book Club Questions

Acknowledgments

WHY THIS BOOK?

Is there a womb in your life? One that's not sure it wants to be filled? *Still No Kids & Still Ok* gives you a glimpse of what that could mean. A womb with a view. Or maybe you've made the childfree choice and reviewing the reasons is a cheeky little hobby. You may even have a beloved little one at home and reading this book will remind you of why that childfree person in your life just doesn't always get you. And vice versa.

This book looks at the childfree choice with a laugh because humor jostles the mind and opens it to ideas. Humor is a tasty purée of philosophy, memoir, and whimsy. And laughter is a joy. Especially when someone is laughing and they just drank milk.

There are plenty of writers, scholars, comedians, and Tik-Tokkers with breasts that somehow defy gravity who have tackled the childfree choice. *Still No Kids* is different because it comes from me, an intentionally childfree oldster with over six decades in the pockets of my stretchable slacks. And don't even ask about my breasts and gravity.

My book *Cheerfully Childless*, created in 2001 with artist Loretta Gomez, was the first humor book solely based on the childfree decision. Happily the childfree theme is now a thing, along with timeless comedy about quirky relationships, old people, and anything having to do with poop.

A pause now for a note on the word "childless." After the release of *Cheerfully Childless*, I got an earful about that word. People used their potty mouths on the subject. Comments ran along these lines:

> "Hey asswipe! The accepted term for those who deliberately choose to not have children is *childfree*."

Ok. That was pretty much the only comment, multiplied a hundred kajillion times, with asswipe being the gentlest word used to describe me. So childfree it is.

WHY THIS BOOK?

We've Come a Long Way, Baby!

I puff up my not-so-perky chest when noting that *Cheerfully Childless* was an early entry in the the childfree oeuvre. But more sophisticated books quickly followed. Those books are edgy, a tad cruel, and make *Cheerfully Childless* seem like something Mrs. Brady doodled while the eight kids in the den fought over the three TV channels. My writing style has matured, though the Brady Bunch tinge is still there (if Mrs. Brady had a potty mouth) since that's me.

Though we've made a lot of progress, society still doesn't fully embrace the no-kid decision. Many people still see a pregnant woman as blessed, while I see her as someone who got laid and got just the result that nature intended. And I hope the sex was great!

Before we proceed, here's one *by the way.*

> By the way, if you felt unloved as a child, this book is not about you. You are amazing. Yes, I'm talking about you.

Cheerfully Choosing

While writing *Cheerfully Childless*, I wondered if the book could shove potentially great parents off the toy-strewn path. Now I know that each person, somehow, makes this intensely personal choice in their own way.

Yes, choice. It's something we all get to make. You know the *Childfree Choice Cheer*, right? No? Well, here it is, though when you hear the Dallas Cowboys cheerleaders do it, with their beaming faces aglow, it's even better.

> *C! is for Childfree Me Me Me!*
> *H! is for Hell No, I Won't Glow!*
> *O! is for Oh, Don't Make Me Watch Disney Movies!*
> *I! is for I Think Nieces and Nephews and Other Random Children are Enough!*
> *C! is for Crap, Just Enjoy Your Own Kids, ok?*
> *E! is for Parenthood is for EVER!*
> *What does it spell?* **CHOICE!**
> *What does it mean?* **Don't fucking do anything unless it's right for you!**

When the Dallas gang jumps in the air and shouts that last line, *it is magic.*

1. WHY BE CHILDFREE?

With my 50th birthday now in the rearview mirror, I'm just as likely to get pregnant as I am to grow antlers. Of course, having sex would help. To grow a child, that is, not antlers. Let's just say, with or without sex, antlers are way more possible at this point.

People often share theories with me on why I chose to be childfree. Being raised in a "dysfunctional" family is a favorite culprit. It's true that my childhood was more Jerry Springer than Oprah, but three of my siblings shared that same Den of Hell and still managed to produce seven offspring between them. My damaged little family has done its part in populating the world.

The absence of warm and fuzzy in my upbringing probably affected me, but it could also be in my DNA. As a kid, the only dolls I loved were Betsy Wetsy (how cool is a peeing doll?), Drowsy (a delightful talking doll that whines when you pull her string!), and Barbie (since my friends and I could dye her hair and create sexual encounters with Ken or Midge or GI Joe). Stuffed animals have such weird button eyes so I said no thank you to them. No, my favorite things to do as a kid were playing Footsie (look up "1970's Footsie toy"), jumping rope, making Barbie have sex, reading, and dreaming about being a grown-up.

Mama Me? Oy!

I've lost count of how many times I've been told, "You would have been a wonderful mother!" A big WTF flashes in my mind. What do I do that spells mama material? I haven't strangled anyone, even when they tell me how empty my life is without kids, which is super good. I embarrass friends when I extemporaneously sing a John Denver song. I know big words ("extemporaneously") and I excel in non-sequiturs. All good mommy stuff?

Maybe it's my sweet old gal vibe which says to some people kids, kids, kids, the more the better, preferably in a room absolutely stuffed with them. So I'm here to tell you: that vibe is in your mind.

1. WHY BE CHILDFREE?

When it comes to children, my level of incompetence is legendary. I once froze up and literally came to a stand-still at a birthday party because a child asked me to cut him a piece of cake. Being more of a help-yourself hostess, I stood, confused, as other fidgety children lined up behind him. *Do I ask each kid how big a piece they want? Will my moral compass let me serve a kid a chunk of sugar with sugar on it? What if the knife slips and I stab myself in the eye?* The cake-hungry child stared at me, licking his upper lip as he watched me do nothing. Luckily, my puzzled mom-friend, wondering why the hell there was a problem, ninja'd in front of me and sliced pieces for that kid and the next 5, no questions asked. I realized it wasn't tough, but I can't say it won't be just as nerve-wracking the next time. When I'm amazing with children, it's a great big accident.

It could be that I'm seen as a Maybe-Mamma since I sometimes babysit. The truth is that mercy is my motivator when it comes to babysitting. I'm a sucker for a parent who weakly whispers to me, "please?" I'll confess it's surprising when I end up having a to-ally Ok time when I babysit. Of course, I also have a totally Ok time in bars, but I don't aspire to be either a bartender or a drunk.

Some loved ones think I would have been a great mom since their kids come back from Ellen-outings and say, "I had an AWESOME time! When can I see Ellen again?" This is because I buy them things. (Sugary things.) Things they want. (More sugary things.) Things that any sane parent would never buy them. (You get the drift.) Things that engage them and keep my participation level low, including movies, plays, amusement parks, and sugary things. This strategy works for occasional outings, but if you do it too often you'll go bankrupt and gain a lot of weight.

By the way. If my beloved nieces and nephews are reading this, I'm not talking about you, of course. Our outings are different and special!

As an aunt, I do more than buy stuff. I also accidentally entertain nieces and nephews when I use the word fuck over and over and then apologize for using the word fuck over and over. The children also enjoy it when I dub them my least shitty niece or nephew of the week. I know how to make kids smile.

It's taken years of hearing comedians rag on about crazy Uncle Jake or whacky Aunt Mimi for me to realize: Wait. Mimi is me-me. I AM the delusional aunt who wears punkish clothes to a concert and thinks, "Boy, I

1. WHY BE CHILDFREE?

look great." I AM the anxious aunt who endlessly gives unrequested advice. ("You should go to college.") I AM the intrusive aunt who spouts commentary on everyone else's life. (You *really* should go to college.") In other words, I'm a crappy parent in aunt's clothing.

As a step-to-the-plate kind of person, I guess I would have been an adequate parent. But only just. I envision myself saying "Mommy will be right out," as I slip into the bathroom and quietly keen, many times a day. This is assuming I could enter a bathroom on my own. New parents tell me that alone time in this special little room is rare, tough, and miraculous.

If I'd had a child, would I have been Mommy Dearest? Mother Teresa? Moms Mabley? Would I have developed that remarkable child/parent bond that puts Gorilla Glue to shame? I don't know.

What I do know is that when I consider how life might have been even more rewarding, a child is not in the fantasy. Instead, I imagine correcting work/life imbalance more quickly, making more effort to buy great knee-high boots, and being less stupid a lot sooner. But I do not imagine laying in a maternity ward with someone yelling at me to PUSH.

1. WHY BE CHILDFREE?

Choosing the Right Curtain

There are so many crucial decisions in life. Apple or Android? Ryan Reynolds or Ryan Gosling? Have children or not?

Luckily there are lots of decision-making tools to choose from. Meditation. Conversation. Cocktails. Weed. Exercise. Squeezing your eyes shut really tight and letting someone else decide. That last one is really popular.

So how do you decide if parenting is right for you? For big decisions, I create lists. I made a pro/con list when deciding to continue a career in radio or switch professions. (Switched profession!) I did it when I considered uprooting from the east to move west. (Moved west!) I did a small quick one when thinking about strangling the whiny kid a few seats back on an airplane. (Did not strangle!)

With lists, you write out the decision plusses and minuses, and one side always becomes longer. The caveat is that it's hard to be honest about the most personal decisions. Using the list technique to decide if you should stay with an insane but crazy-adorable partner, for example, can end up with reams of paper and weird reasons for staying with your screwed-up sweetie. (Leave!)

The same problem with self-honesty may happen on baby-or-not lists. But give it a try. If "the little shits just annoy me" is on the con side, ask yourself if "MY little shits won't annoy me," is an honest item for the pro side. Keep it real and the list should help.

If there had been a sci-fi-no-fertility-humanity-dying-out-scenario during my childbearing years, I would have been a good citizen of Earth, schtupping like crazy in an abandoned missile silo. But I hear tell that populating the earth is not a problem.

When I'm told, "You would have been a great mom," I know it's a compliment. Frazzled parents say this after I do one smart thing with their kid for twenty seconds. Like telling the kid I find their artwork marvelous (which I do) or letting their kid put fifty braids in my hair, all at different angles (I have a picture of this and I look awesome.) After that tiny bit of brilliant pseudo-parenting, I am a hero.

But I can't sustain great mommyness. It's true I'm not a nasty bitch in public. But how about in private, when I don't get alone time precisely when I want it? When my cat dares to ask for pets when I'm eating a snacky on the couch? If I'd had kids, would I have learned to be more spontaneous? Find joy in things that seem totally not joyful? Been a great mom? Who the hell knows? My guess is no.

When people ask if I wish I'd had children, I get that feeling you have after stepping on a slug barefoot. It's annoying and yucky. That describes my lizard brain reaction to the Kid Question. Or maybe a slug brain reaction, since the slug, now disemboweled between my toes, is also gloomy. Either way, this response tells me I'm hardwired to be childfree. I suspect I'm not alone.

1. WHY BE CHILDFREE?

In part, I don't have children because my brain has a superpower. It tunes out things that might make me act like a responsible adult. For example, I was showing my fabulous retro shirt to a friend when her face transformed into a mask of fear. She ran! Wow, did she hate my shirt that much? Bad juju connected to Paisley?

Nope. She ran because her nearby baby was *shrieking*. I did not hear it. At all. This I-didn't-hear-it superpower is perfect after the question "Who wants to volunteer?" or "Who can carve the turkey?" Not great for child-rearing.

Parents assure me that if I had a kid, I'd be attuned to their screaming. Maybe. In the 1980's I was a DJ at WPST in Princeton playing (or so said the radio station tagline) "The Best Music!" I was in the studio alone, loving the glorious segueway I created with *Like a Virgin* fading and blending into *Walk Like an Egyptian*. What I could not hear were the visitors outside the studio door repeating my name and rapping on the door for five minutes. The sound finally penetrated and I shrieked. Then they shrieked.

My poor hearing could be the culprit, but I think it's more that I disappear inside my unending thoughts and my ears take a vacation. *Not a useful parenting quality.*

MARVELOUS QUOTE #1

"On the threshold of thirty and divorce, the personable daughter of a Southern Baptist minister once calmly informed me that any child of hers would probably be a battered child. She was being neither neurotic nor more self-centered than people usually are, merely honest about her strong preference not to have children."

—**Christopher Clausen, from "Child-free in Toyland" in *The American Scholar***

There are those people who always knew they wanted children; those who knew they didn't; and a huge number who have no fucking clue. So why do people choose to be childfree? Glad you asked!

1. WHY BE CHILDFREE?

Reasons People Choose to Be Childfree

- **Disinterest.** These people considered the option and thought "meh."
- **One partner doesn't want them.** Yikes. Find that out before you commit! That compatibility question is right up there with the answer to "Tattoos, yes, or tattoos, no?" and "Love or don't love Downton Abbey?"
- **They know their child tolerance threshold.** Children sometimes: totally fab. Children all the time: holy shit.
- **They don't believe stupid stuff people tell them.** Such as: "It's different when it's your child."
- **They have ample children in their life.** These are teachers, daycare workers, aunts, uncles, and clowns.
- **The sound of children playing is never uplifting.** Never.
- **They just hate children.** Some people just do.

MARVELOUS QUOTE #2

"My mother once asked
'Who will take care of you when
you get old?' and I said,
'Mom, if that's why you had me, you blew it.'

—Lois Betts, from "Three's a Crowd,"
in the *San Diego Union-Tribune*

A Little Help from Myself

I've heard parents say "I hope my children will take care of me when I'm old." This makes me wonder if some parents have children to groom them for handy purposes, like fixing technology, shoveling snow, or being a bulletproof excuse for sick days.

Many who expect their children to be on Geritol-call are those who cared for their own parents. But we don't always reap, in precisely the same manner, what we sow. Before child labor laws, parents could send 8-year-old Junior to a factory to both earn money and escape demon idleness. Nowadays Junior may want room and

1. WHY BE CHILDFREE?

board for years beyond the time his bedroom should have been converted to your Cave of Personal Desires. Or a sewing room. (Maybe the same thing?) Whatever.

In your basement?
You buy his food?
No, ma'am.
Your 50-year-old son is not deductible.

Since my childfree vibes began early, I started to plan for the financial side of caring for myself back when I was more plum and less prune. I considered options.

Option #1: Win the lottery and be amazingly rich.

Option #2: Be a best-selling author and be amazingly rich.

Option #3: Get training or education to ultimately nab a pretty enjoyable job, preferably with benefits, and save money for retirement and health needs.

I pursued option #1 for years, and though I know it's hard to believe, I did not win the lottery. Option #2 brought in enough cash from book sales to buy a car, but I didn't want to live in a car. Eventually, #3 became the solution. It can be done: get a kind of groovy job with benefits. You may not earn enough to upgrade your phone every year, but would your kiddy caretakers have done better?

What about the question of loneliness as you morph over the years from a prune to a stewed prune? If you don't have children, are you afraid you won't have visitors in your old age? Well, you need to reach out and make the effort to make and keep friends and stay connected to siblings, cousins, and such. And also try not to be a shit.

1. WHY BE CHILDFREE?

I Only Wanna Be with Me

I don't need constant company. My ratio for needing to be alone vs. being with others is is around 60 alone/40 others. (Maybe 80/20, but I can't even confess that to myself.) While planning a solo car trip to Albuquerque, my sister Sarah, a mother of two, gasped "You're going ALONE?" I know. A sane person would ask, "Why on Earth would you go to Albuquerque?!" (I had a great time. What can I say?) Then you might point out, "This alone thing is not a parent thing. I know some childfree people who also don't like to travel alone." Point taken. But it does seem that alone time is especially terrifying to those with children.

I have a friend who wakes each morning, content in knowing her near-grown child is in bed, sleeping like a dead slug, and will only respond with a barely audible "Yeeeah" after my friend's gentle nagging escalates into yelling. The friend chooses to interpret the "Yeah" as "Love you so much, Mom." Sometimes my friend glances at the now-awake but still half-asleep pre-adult and realizes her sweet baby will soon be mumbling and stumbling in her own home, leaving my friend in a scary and unfamiliar state: being alone. She then makes her daughter heart-shaped pancakes topped with smiley faces.

If I'd had kids, I would have grown accustomed to waking each morning to other people wandering around. But I didn't and I'm not. I don't wake up and think "Dang, I wish someone was in the next room texting with heaven knows who before I bully them out the door to school." As one childfree friend of mine says, "It can be hard to make people believe how much I love my own company."

Parents have learned to stay within caring distance of others. They hang out with humans who stick crayons up their noses, bite the dog, and love leaning out of second-story windows. Caring distance extends to the farthest distance one can move

1. WHY BE CHILDFREE?

where it's still possible to quickly dig out those crayons, comfort the dog, and walk ever so quietly up to a window-leaning child and...save them, of course!

Parents seem to get used to having others around. It may sometimes drive them so crazy that they've found a space behind the washer to crouch behind for like, just an hour. Eventually, they miss the little buggers. Or remember they left the window open.

Though I do crave companionship, my tactic of seeking the company of loved ones, as well as potentially murderous strangers, ensures I have company when I want it. Traveling alone, for example, brings the joy of low-stakes companionship. You hit it off with a stranger on a trip, and you don't need to later watch Hammy, their pet hamster, when they go away. They don't know if you've gained weight. They don't know about your old nose or your new ass. You may even find that someone with stupid political views (that is, views different than yours) is a good companion for day-tripping. It would suck if all relationships were like this. But they're not. These are *vacationships*. They help you feel connected to others while letting you remain pleasantly selfish. Now that's a vacation.

Banish that "how sad" thought you're having! Yes, it can be tough to be alone, but I think we all know we can be alone even when we're with others. Briefly imagining closeness to a random human is no sadder than imagining yourself as the main character in *Fifty Shades of Grey*. I love imagination!

Of course, I get lonely. But I've also felt lonely in a partner's arms. Loneliness is solvable. If you're not constantly cranky, you probably have people in your life who love you. Yeah, they don't want to see you all the time. But would your kids, either?

Am I a typical person? Can I exemplify an everyday person who has rarely changed a poopy diaper and is still ok? Let's look at the evidence.

- **Like others**, I continually gain and lose ten pounds. (I should just carry them in my purse.)
- **Unlike others** who play yoyo with their weight, I won't wear SPANX®.
- **Like others**, I love scary movies.
- But **unlike others**, I watch them in tiny chunks, over many days, since they terrify me.
- **Like others**, I enjoy some desserts.

1. WHY BE CHILDFREE?

- But **unlike others**, I hate the taste of pie. Even your mom's famous apple pie.
- **Unlike others**, I hate bacon, (yeah, shut up, bacon lovers).
- And also, **unlike others**, I love broccoli (yeah, shut up, broccoli-haters).
- **Like others**, after years of working, I was able to buy a home.
- But **unlike others**, the phrase "living large" has little meaning to me since "living small" seems fine, as in small house and small car. (No kids, remember?)
- **Unlike others**, I can't stand those theoretically comfortable reclining theater seats.
- I'm pretty sure I'm **unlike all others** in this and that this is weird.
- **Like others**, I get a goofy grin on my face after a hug from a toddler.
- But **unlike others**, I also get a goofy grin on my face when I do absolutely nothing.
- I'm often **simultaneously delighted and bored**.
- Not sure if this is common.

It seems, on balance, I'm normal enough.

Money Can't Buy Me Kids

When I choose a romantic partner, I don't think about their "earning power." Though front-row theater seats and seats behind home plate would be nice, I'd rather have a partner who's willing to get off his seat and look charmingly uncoordinated on a dance floor. This means love has brought me emotional, rather than actual, riches.

So. Is it more Ok for the childfree to be life-rich and cash-poor than parents? Nah. Anything cherished is likely worth the cost. I've seen low-money parents live delightful lives. The phrases "on sale" and "that can be fixed" are sacred in these households. If you're considering a child in your life, am I saying you shouldn't worry about child-rearing expenses? No. If you don't consider those expenses, you're a bonehead, and my surely correct assumption here is that you're not.

If having a child means the world to you, just know that the cost of raising a child is similar in concept to getting a hair blowout. It's pricey and not essential, but you know you look FREAKING FABULOUS with that blowout so of course it's worth it! If you're not the CEO of an over-valued start-up and you're considering a child, just also consider if you can live with fewer Caribbean jaunts. Or at least not in your own jet.

All Your Fault!

Here's a passage from the 1891 book *Hints on Child Training*, by H. Clay Trumbull:

> It is, therefore, largely a child's training that settles the question of whether a child is graceful or awkward in his personal movements, gentle or rough in his ways with his fellows; whether he is methodical and precise, or unsystematic and irregular in the discharge of his daily duties, whether he is industrious or indolent in his habits; whether the tastes which he indulges in his diet and dress and reading and amusements and companionships are refined, or are low. In all these things his course indicates what his training has been; or it suggests the training that he needed, but has missed.

1. WHY BE CHILDFREE?

So, in short, parents are responsible for anything their child does, ever. You make them brilliant, or you fuck them up. It's true that I'm quoting a book over a century out-of-date, but that thinking is in action today.

When friends who are parents share fears that they're not raising their children as well as (fill in other stupid parents' names here) I remind them, like everything in life, there are countless excellent ways to help your wild little flower bloom. But I guess the niggling feeling of ultimate responsibility must be tough to put in perspective when your job is to raise another human being. And everyone feels free to evaluate your job performance. Whether other parents are dispensing actual unasked-for advice or sharing disapproving glances, the message is clear: "They are better parents than you are."

Here's an excerpt from Bo Burnham's special, *Bo Burnham: Words, Words, Words*

> "The princess fairy tales teach young girls such important lessons. You know, like Cinderella. It doesn't matter where you come from or how poor you are as long as you're incredibly hot."

If I had given birth to a little angel child, I sometimes wonder how I might have tackled tough topics with them. Like why women scream for help in porn videos. Or why repulsive politicians do things that would put my cherub in a Time-Out. And how some people think they must paint their delightfully-colored walls white when they sell a house. As I think about these questions, I fall into a coma-like state. These questions are so hard! I guess I would have risen to each occasion by researching each concept and talking to experts, friends, and family. I would have taken a deep breath and readied myself for a difficult, but important, parent/kid discussion.

Wait, no.

The truth is, I'm pretty sure I would have just passed out. Even thinking about all that stuff almost made me pass out.

This fall into oblivion doesn't happen when adults ask me for advice. *Is it Ok to drop an overbearing friend? Can I recommend a bingeable series?* Maybe adults are easier when it comes to advice because I know my comments may be helpful or neutral in the moment, as opposed to being a potential life-long building block. (Pretty sure I never fucked up anyone by recommending they drop the asshole friend and watch *The Good Place*.)

1. WHY BE CHILDFREE?

I'm probably elevating the impact an adult has on a child. Becoming a parent doesn't automatically make one wise, and children of unwise people make their way in the world. I do have one indisputable truth to share with young and old alike: If you sell your house, and you have beautiful colorful walls, don't paint them white.

MARVELOUS QUOTE #3

> "If your kid needs a role model and you ain't it, you're both fucked."

— George Carlin, from his book *Brain Droppings*

Ask Me if I Care?

As a childfree oldster, it's lovely to have things I don't need to care about. I don't care if a "good" school is nearby. I don't care if the closest thing I have to a playground is The Electric Cure pub featuring a jocular satanic style. I'm rather pleased that my little town of Edgewater is known for its superb marijuana dispensaries. I enjoy carelessly displaying knick-knacks in my home with small detachable pieces just waiting to be swallowed. If my friend's children hear me say naughty words they're sure to repeat, I can only say sorry. (They'll be ok.)

Despite being a kidless crone, I still want all schools to be good, I want lots of playgrounds with non-detachable parts, and I'd love to see children as fluent in expressive language as they are in emojis. There are some some things I care a lot about.

1. WHY BE CHILDFREE?

Multiply Something Else

I avoid wading into religious waters, but since this entire book sort of does that anyway, I'm taking the plunge. Let's look at the phrase, "Be fruitful and multiply." Is it really saying to endlessly multiply new humans? If taken literally, I think a sensible higher being would add a P.S. that says, "Uh, you can slow down. I figured you would get that."

There are plenty of great things in this world to work at fruitfully multiplying. Consideration. BTS Boys. Fart jokes. Logic. Does it just have to be squirmy little babies?

Ah, the pressure to procreate. If it's not the Lord, then it's relatives. If it's not relatives, it's friends or co-workers or movies starring adorable children like that *Home Alone* kid. And if it's not the cute *Home Alone* kid or sweet little Ralphie in *A Christmas Story*, it's ourselves, acknowledging it's more common than not to make babies.

Of course, you already know societal norms and choices don't always make sense. Society is just dandy with some weird stuff. For example, these things are all seen as ok:

- The belief we can lose weight if we just eat when we're hungry.

- Child-care workers earning less than the hosts of *The Great British Baking Show*.
- Revering a sport that routinely results in brain injury.
- The popularity of vehicles so large you need to leap into them.
- Venerating children with sentimental words while opposing the expansion of options that support parental needs.
- Butt strip bikini waxing. (And if you didn't know, sorry to share that.)

Here's hoping that those considering procreation can follow their desires, whatever they may be. Closing their eyes really, really tightly and letting someone else decide is totally not recommended.

MARVELOUS QUOTE #4

"This is the age of the life hack, the bucket list, and that greedy phrase 'having it all.' So, the question becomes, 'Will a child enhance that ride or derail it?'"

—Sanjiv Bhattacharya, from "Kids Aren't Us" in *Esquire*

1. WHY BE CHILDFREE?

Who You Calling Selfish?

Long ago and far away, as a 16-year-old Sears employee, my plan to be forever childfree came up in a chat with a co-worker among the polyester slack racks. My fellow clothes straightener, also 16, asked "Have you always been so selfish?" At the time I considered the question. *Was* I selfish? Had I been a self-centered wretch for the first 192 months of my life? At the time, I didn't know the answer.

Fast forward multiple decades and I've had a chance to consider that question. (Which is why I'm not great with spitfire-fast social media exchanges. Instead of needing seconds to respond, I need decades.)

I've learned selfishness is a matter of perception. For example, I think You're Being Selfish since you won't let me sip your delicious pumpkin spice latte, available only during the holidays, and so especially desirable. You think You're Not Being Selfish since you know I'll just moan about the calories and then my sip will be half the latte.

People may think I'm Being Selfish for not shouldering a fair share of child nurturing, while I may think they're Really Selfish because their family's needs take precedence over the nurturing needs of all other living things. Including me. Wah.

Some people choose jobs with unselfishness baked into them. Doctors, who heal us; engineers who create safe structures; and WWF wrestlers, because they are rippling oiled muscles of greatness. All these professions make the world better, none appeal to everyone, and you're not selfish if you choose instead to be a drag queen. (Though they're neat, too, so good choice!)

One person's selfishness is somebody else's hard-earned pumpkin latte. **The reality is that you will be judged for any decision you make ever, ever.** Even if you make your decision using moral and ethical standards and routinely save puppies from harm.

In her book *Child-free by Choice*, Amy Blackstone notes that parents with one child are labeled selfish, as are those with many children. Selfish because you have kids? Selfish because you don't? There just ain't no making everyone happy. Especially mama.

I do think that being childfree makes me lazier, which I guess could be equated with selfishness. For example, I don't care if my lettuce isn't washed. I throw that

1. WHY BE CHILDFREE?

sludge on the plate and eat it. But if friends are coming to dinner, Martha Stewart stand aside. I'd rent a power washer to clean those filthy greens. It feels natural to take the extra step and pick out the bugs when another person is involved. Is this how parents feel about caring for their children? Maybe.

Here's an aside for parents and would-be parents when it comes to selfless financial generosity. The kids don't always want the extravagant support you offer. If an adult offspring who bought 50 super-nice creams on Sephora for the cost of a car down payment says they want emotional support as they deal with creditors, and not your retirement savings, *they might mean it!* (Ok, at that moment they would love you for throwing cash their way. But they'll figure it out if you don't.) If the now-grown kid does, in fact, want your retirement savings, remember there are other options. That retirement moolah is meant for mai tai's and beach time. (You earned it, dammit!) It will help if you imagine the child as a responsible adult and not the apple-cheeked rascal who sweetly peed on you the second you removed his diaper.

I do sort of get it. When we love someone, it's easy to do the selfless thing, every time. Over and over. Just keep this important thing in mind: mai tai's are absolutely delicious.

1. WHY BE CHILDFREE?

MARVELOUS QUOTE #5

Couples without children are always shown [in auto ads] preparing for parenthood. They're decorating the nursery, trading in the car for a minivan. Just once I'd like to see someone trading in the SUV and buying a Corvette."

—Maria Bareiss, from "Childless by Choice" in *American Demographics*

Ain't Nobody's Business but My Own

I follow the life philosophy captured in the aphorism "Don't complain and don't explain." Here's how I interpret that phrase and sorry it doesn't rhyme. The don't complain means we need to do tough but practical shit all the time and it saves brain cells to get on and do it. This doesn't mean we should never bitch and moan, since we should do that all the louder when it matters. (Tip: It rarely matters.)

The "don't explain" part is the lovely bit. Some people feel compelled to justify every decision or action. This results in explanations no one wants to hear, lying, or sharing stuff that's nobody's damn business. An example is the question, "Aw! Why don't you come to the party?" The answer closest to the truth could be, "I just don't fucking feel like it." The G-rated version would be, "Not this time, but thanks a lot for asking." (Or sound like an old gal and say, "I'm sending my regrets this time.")

There are times when giving a reason is a decent thing to do, like explaining why you were snort-laughing on your phone during a funeral. Otherwise, "don't explain" makes life happier. I apply this method to the question, "Didn't you want children?" My answer is, "Not this time, but thanks a lot for asking."

Things You Can Do With Pets, Not Kids #1

Use money on continuing education for yourself, not them.

Doggy Do U.
- Making your natural mouth look even more like a smile
- Frisbees 101: Mastering the gentle hold
- Beyond Balls and Slippers: Other things to Fetch
- The Head Tilt: How and when For maximum "cute"

E. Metter

2. CONCEPTION IS STILL A THING

Society has some expectations that most of us agree on. If a dog poops on a sidewalk, the sidewalk will be stinky. So, *no crapping on the sidewalk* is a splendid norm to follow! But what about other expectations? Say, procreation?

If you're among the surging wave of people who say, "Hell no, I won't glow," I'll bet you've gotten questions about your choice from others. Maybe also within yourself. Though everyone has an opinion on what color you painted your living room ("Oh, I never would have chosen such a bold color!"), it's not as fraught as the choice to embrace or ignore childbirth. Few other decisions prompt such deep soul-searching. It's right up there with choosing a mate (if you want one), selecting a career (to avoid cardboard as a home construction material), and picking sprinkles, Reese's,

2. CONCEPTION IS STILL A THING

gummies, or all three at the frozen yogurt place. These are all important choices, but none have the label "instinct" attached.

Strong urges do seem to drive humans. Could it be that different natural impulses are scattered throughout the species for balance? For example, some extroverted people crave attention, which gives us celebrities and former royalty, while others prefer anonymity, which gives us a break from those fucking extroverts. Some people hate to slide down mountains strapped to slippery boards, while others revel in potential death by doing just that. And so, it follows that some people want children, so we keep the species going, and some don't, to give us all some damn breathing room.

Nature definitely likes us to screw around. There were many decades when it was pretty much all I aspired to. Virtually every decision was based on the possibility of having sex with someone. Nature is super into procreation. Of course, nature also lets humans develop big brains to invent glorious things like penicillin, pizza, and contraception. Thank you, nature! Thank you, big brains!

MARVELOUS QUOTE #6

"Another question I always get, particularly with the posh papers, the Sundays, doing a profile piece, and they're still trying to alienate you and make you look different, and they always say things like, "You don't have children." I say, "No." They say, "Why don't you have children?" Which is a really odd question to ask someone, "Why DON'T you have children?" as opposed to asking people, "Why DO you have children?"

—**Ricky Gervais, from his show**
Ricky Gervais: Humanity

I do have a protective urge that might be called an instinct. I'm a blubbery mess when I read that a child's been hurt, neglected, or deprived of Beatles music. (C'mon. That music spans generations.) If the point is to continue a species, this protective instinct is brilliant. When humans aren't yet developed physically, emotionally, or morally, humans further along the development curve can guide them and make sure they've heard *While My Guitar Gently Weeps*. Even a remake.

2. CONCEPTION IS STILL A THING

Grown humans can also use their big lumbering bodies to protect youngsters. If someone gave me the choice between sparing my life and that of any child, my no-brainer response would be "Point that bazooka at me, Sylvester." Children deserve to grow up and have a shot at life, even if most squander the chance horribly.

What exactly is a biologically driven urge? Can we tell the difference between the feeling nature inspires and the inspiration from Pampers "Pooface" baby commercial? (Their word, not mine. Apparently, this is the face of a diaper-wearing baby who just pooped.)

Have you ever had the impulse to lean across a meeting table and slap a colleague? Don't do it! Urges should not always be followed.

The matter of instinct, related to the childfree choice, boils down to the question, "Is there something *wrong* with those who don't want to have children?" Hell, yeah. As wrong as reveling in extended alone time. As wrong as liking ONLY the first two Star Wars movies. As wrong as staying in bed until 10am when you got in there at 9pm. As wrong as re-gifting every gift. As wrong as preferring a movie's edited version over the Director's Cut. As wrong as watching children's science shows to learn science stuff. As wrong as crushing on a BTS boy one-third your age. (Speaking for a friend.) As wrong as both loving and hating Arnold Schwarzenegger. As wrong as never answering phone calls. As wrong as only really cleaning your house when people are coming over. As wrong as singing *I'm too Sexy* in the shower. Or anywhere. As wrong as jogging for ten seconds and then walking the rest of the way. Definitely, absolutely, *wrong*.

Things You Can Do With Pets, Not Kids #2

Have an unconditionally loving teenager.

2. CONCEPTION IS STILL A THING

In college, a billion years ago, I lived with 13 young women in an off-campus house that used to be a convent. (Yes, a place that nuns called home. You can't make this stuff up. A 90-year-old retired priest was our landlord.) I can't tell you how often one of my Convent sisters spent days jumping up and down because they weren't ready for the child they may have created while out and about and in and out. I'm still stunned by anyone playing reproduction roulette when they don't even know if they want a child. For me, it was never worth the *agita* to take the chance.

In my 20s, I was thrilled to go on a date with a dishy guy from a local Greek restaurant. Being a wanton tart, I was ready to bed this hottie on the first date. Until he said he wouldn't wear a condom. He was enraged by my insistence. (Be sure you hear a Greek accent when you read his reply!) "In my country, only prostitutes demand condoms!" I told him he was in my country and in my bedroom. Rather than covering up and plunging into the wonders of my cute self, he left. Eating some baklava quickly cheered me up.

I should have asked Restaurant Guy, "Would you be excited if I call you in a month to say you and I will soon be parents? After our one-night stand and semi-forgetting me, will you drop to one knee and say (remember accent!) "My love! You have created a child! You are magic! I shall be your partner forever and we will live an enchanted life on Santorini with our little blessing!" Based on my limited acquaintance with Restaurant Guy, my guess is he actually would have said, "Take care of it. And what's your name again?"

How Do They Do It?

I view parenting with awe. Child-rearing seems like flying a Boeing jumbo jet with squirrels in your hair. Or convincing a New Yorker there's decent theater in Denver. Very hard to do!

I look at parenting as an extreme sport: full-throttle dedication no matter the agony; heavenly highs that can't be matched in other ways; and random people yelling at you to do better. Though that all sounds exhilarating, I'll stick with biking really slowly.

I also hold other people in awe. Like activists who sacrifice quiet contentment to further social justice. Or nursing home caregivers who put up with Mr. Jones saying a

2. CONCEPTION IS STILL A THING

hundred times "If I said you had a great body would you hold it against me?" Or women with those goddamn bouncy breasts.

But no one awes me more than parents who seem sane and upright despite having teenagers at home. The parent/teen relationship is so obvious in horror movie tropes that I wonder if teens are the actual inspiration for them.

. . .*A spider with a hundred legs* (teen) *springs out* (oh, didn't they tell you?) *and binds you in an unbreakable web* (after-school activities and weekend sports.)

. . .*You're trapped in a spinning, nausea-inducing maze* (teen bedroom.)

. . .*A misshapen shadow is lurking around the corner! You know it will change your world in horrible ways* (your daughter's boyfriend.)

. . .*A sinister, confusing symbol appears* (your child's first tattoo.)

Stephen King is a great horror writer. He also raised three teenagers. Coincidence?

When it comes to admiring parents, even children do it. I have friends who see their parents as best friends. Their parents steered them through childhood with humor, grace, practical wisdom, and a sprinkling of sarcasm. They rarely voiced regret at giving birth to them. They didn't blink when their child said they were gay, non-binary, or (take your pick) liberal or conservative. They faltered just slightly when they learned their baby hated Beatles music. If you think you'd be like those parents, procreating could be for you.

Of course, you can be deeply moved by child/parent relationships and still feel fine with no little peeps in the nest. The singer Pink appeared on an awards program swinging on a trapeze, joyfully entwined with her six-year-old daughter. As parent and child grinned at each other I turned into a big maudlin puddle enjoying this intensely loving display. But I still don't blame my lazy womb for depriving me of mid-air embraces. I know myself, and I would definitely fall off that trapeze. And miss the net.

It's True That Kids are Essential

I'm putting out a hope to the universe that there are people who know they want to raise children, will love

2. CONCEPTION IS STILL A THING

it, and do it well. Why? After living a decently long time now (some might say indecently), I know there are reasons why children are vitally important.

Reasons Children are Important

- Nothing is cuter than a four-year-old dancing.
- You can always start a conversation with a parent by asking about their child.
- Dolly Parton was a kid once which proves kids can evolve into great adults.
- New humans bring new perspectives, inventions, and ideas that may improve life quality worldwide. Or they may hold awesome parties I get to attend.
- Children might be deeply fulfilling for some people since I've heard that.
- Third-grade school plays featuring kids playing Jesus are charming and free.
- Some great causes, like the *Help Children Who Hate Stuffed Animals Charity*, are supported because children are affected.
- Little children don't see old people as unattractive. They see us as Muppets.

- We need extreme fitness instructors who bring us to the point of death.
- The littlest tykes are the only humans not posting selfies.
- I want old people to stop asking the bar band to play *Stairway to Heaven*.
- Young folks may do something about societal problems I only bitch about.
- We all need people who make horrible and naive life choices early in their lives so we oldsters can feel wise.

My advanced years have also made me privy to fantastical motives for having a child. So, I'm also putting out a wish that no one chooses to have children for these reasons.

Dumb Reasons People Have Children

- They think babies are cute.
- Their parents or a partner demands it.
- They're told a higher power demands it.
- Their stellar genes need to be passed on for the good of civilization. (Gag.)
- Their friend had a way fun baby shower.

2. CONCEPTION IS STILL A THING

- They think a child will save a massively struggling relationship. Spoiler: *It won't.*
- Their friend with a child excludes them and hangs with other parents. (Relax. You'll make new, childfree friends, and the ones with children will be back.)

MARVELOUS QUOTE #7

"If someone asks why I don't want children it usually ends with me saying: 'As long as I prefer to have a dog to a baby, I shouldn't have children. Period.' You can't argue with that. So that's usually the most efficient [reply.]"

— Interviewee Eva From "Why Would You Want a Baby When You Could Have a Dog?" in *Social Science*

There are crappy pet owners. The people who don't understand that a cat's claws are specifically designed to shred your couch, your old LP covers, and you. The people who don't understand that a dog cannot just scamper up and use your indoor toilet. These people can probably scare up a new owner for their sad pet, but that's not an option when the baby is human. Neither is going to a maternity ward to ask, "May I return this? It's not working out."

For those thinking about having a baby, it could be useful to think about "having a person." Saying *person* is a reminder that your squirmy bundle of giggling cuteness will one day be a plain old farting adult. If that scenario sounds peachy, then I can't wait to attend your baby shower. Just wait 'til you see what I can make with toilet paper!

Give the Kid a Break, but Not a Frosé

As a childfree person, I sometimes forget that children are childlike. A friend and I were outdoors at the airy, bustling Edgewater Beer Garden, enjoying frosés. Two little tykes ate dinner at the other end of our picnic table while the parents socialized at a nearby table. (Parents can be so smart!)

One of our tablemates, around 5, walked to our end of the table and asked, "Do you two have grandchildren?" I first thought, "What? We're so young! How could we have grandchildren?" But there's no fooling children. They know Muppets when they see them. "Yes," I said.

2. CONCEPTION IS STILL A THING

"We have kitty children." "Four-footed-furry children," added my companion. The child considered this, swept her hands down her torso, then asked, "Do you have children that look like me? "Ohh," I said. "Ohh," my friend said. We pretended to consider. "HUMAN children," we mused. "No," we concluded. "None of those."

At first, it annoyed me that this innocent little human thought a great first question for her new Muppet buddies should be, "Have you given birth?" Did her parents teach her that each adult is matched by at least one child?

I decided to give the kid a break since her life is more about parents, grandparents, and teachers rather than ideas, hobbies, or any logical curiosity about whether my frosé tastes good. I realize the child was actually being social, looking for a point of commonality. I guess I could lighten up and appreciate that it would have been tougher if she'd asked for a sip of my frosé.

2. CONCEPTION IS STILL A THING

It's Gonna Be Great!

I'm told child-rearing is ultimately rewarding. As in: "Sure! Raising children can be hard, but ultimately, wow, it's worth it!" But the thing is, we don't need to pursue everything that could be rewarding.

Since my mommy ship has sailed, done some sightseeing, partied all night, thrown up, and sunk, I embrace the ultimately rewarding choices I still have in my old lady life. Such as nourishing healthy relationships and starving sick ones. Or spontaneous trips to Albuquerque. Or enjoying high-volume emotional or mental breakdowns with no witnesses. Or being happily clueless when it comes to just how much an open bar at a wedding will cost. Ultimately, I feel pretty rewarded.

Like Father Like Son?

Children may carry on your name. How cool to someday see your family name on a high school sports trophy! Or the Honor Roll! Or in a large font on an FBI Wanted poster.

Have no fear, childfree comrades! Your name can also endure. People will see it as they shield their eyes from the sun glinting off the brass plaque immortalizing your support of a marvelous cause. Your name will live on through the wisdom you passed on to others ("Ok, if not college, how about an apprenticeship?") Your name will be spoken with reverence as your nephew uses the stone hash pipe you gave him which should last forever. Ample proof you do not need a child for your legacy to to be assured.

To those who feel they owe it to society to have children because their genes are spectacular, I'd say, just quit it. There's no guarantee a child will inherit the best genes on offer. Even if they do, they might use those gifts to cure cancer, or they may use them to create sci-fi movie effects. (Ok, which is pretty awesome, so maybe a good reason to have a child.) Or they may use those gifts to feel superior to others and be a general pain in the ass. You just don't know. If gifting the world your qualities is your sole reason for procreation, maybe just gift yourself instead.

Population Implosion

Babies can be like little fusion reactions. Ka-bloom. Suddenly you're a nuclear family. Some newly exploded families become so inwardly focused that the great big world bashing at their bubble is virtually unseen. Sure, you can kind of blurrily see other non-essential beings out there. But who cares?

I won't deny there's something special about family relationships. They help me learn to get along with those I would normally ignore, sue, or plot against. (Not you, family member who is reading this! A different family member.)

Two people in a relationship may be seen as only a couple, but a couple with a baby is a family. But there are other routes to dandy families. With a little effort, you can make friends who are like family. I may value non-family relations more than family ties since I work a little more for them. Though I try to treat relatives like friends and not take their love for granted, it's tough to lose blood relations no matter what the hell you do. Maybe this adds security to family relationships, but it's also irritating. I've had relatives who decided they could drop all courtesy, be self-absorbed ninnies, and still be loved by playing the family card. I decided to fold on those relationships.

2. CONCEPTION IS STILL A THING

MARVELOUS QUOTE #8

"If I had kids, my kids would hate me... They would have ended up on the equivalent of the *Oprah* show talking about me because something would have had to suffer and it would've probably been them."

— **Oprah Winfrey, from an interview with the *Hollywood Reporter***

Is it Worth the Effort?

We put crazy energy into things we find gratifying. Maybe it's working as a School Board member even though you get yelled at all the time. Or watching every one of the twenty-five thousand *Law & Order* episodes. Or having a kid. But if the satisfaction gained from what you're doing isn't enough, the enthusiasm won't last. With pressure to procreate so rampant, it can be hard to pause and consider whether child-rearing will retain its charming challenge down the road.

We sometimes do things when they feel like the right thing to do. Childbirth should not be in that category. The do-the-right-thing category includes things like:

- Not saying a friend looks hungover.
- Not saying a friend looks more hungover than you've ever seen them.
- Not saying a friend looks so hungover you're afraid they're going to die.
- Cleaning dishes when someone else did the cooking.

As you see, there's no mention of childbirth on the do-the-right-thing list.

So many things we love are the exact things that make other people gag. It may feel natural to drone on about your love of pickleball, Drew Barrymore, or parenthood in the hope of infecting others with your zeal. Resist and desist, my friends! Mentioning and sharing is great, but expecting that everyone can like what you like just gets creepy.

I met a guy who worked in the Peace Corps. In his international travels, he endured drenching rains, scorching heat, rough sleeping conditions, bitey bugs, and only

2. CONCEPTION IS STILL A THING

the slowest progress toward his goals. He was utterly happy. His work objectives so energized him that he didn't mind being a mosquito munchie every night. A young and naïve me said, "It sounds awful, but if you find it so fulfilling, maybe I should look into it." He said, "NO. If you don't feel drawn to it, you'll regret it. And also do a shitty job." He'd seen too many miserable people who joined the Peace Corps because it seemed like **the right thing to do**.

There aren't many things that all people enjoy, so it's good to have a grip on what floats your personal boat before making a lifelong commitment. I can only confidently name one thing everyone loves: breathing. We all agree. Breathing is awesome. At one point I would have said Tom Hanks, but that ship has sailed. So, with universal agreement that we all like different things, why would we all be drawn to having children?

It Just Ain't Easy

Out in public, I see the challenges of parenthood. Like when a parent is dealing with a whiny kid at a supermarket. I've seen parents try to calm little Brewster with firm directives ("Brewster, please use your indoor voice."); with reasoning ("Brewster. Do you hear other people whining?"); and with cajoling ("Brewster! If you

2. CONCEPTION IS STILL A THING

use your indoor voice, yes, you can have the 90-ounce Twix bar. Yes, both sides!")

Sometimes a parent will beat the odds to score one of those ankle-maiming carts that looks like a sportscar and briefly amuses Brewster. When even the sportscar fails, the siren sound of child-whining increases, along with other shoppers' heart rates. The purse-lipped parent stoically continues to shop, shaking their head and making eye contact that says, "YOU try to shut the kid up." I sometimes take the implied dare and engage the little whiner in a diversion ("Wow! Are you a fireman? Is that the sound a firetruck makes?") which sometimes works briefly and breaks the whine cycle. A kid knows how to push their parents' buttons, but a stranger is a big buttonless blob, so better to just shut up. These are the times when being a stranger feels downright cozy.

Teens Can be Handy

I had both terrific friends and nasty tormentors in high school. I was a freak, a brain, and a seriously unconfident kid. The great times included playing drums in the band, smoke breaks on the patio with totally cute guys who were all failing their classes, and having saint-like

2. CONCEPTION IS STILL A THING

teachers who seemed to actually like their students. Living through that once was good, thanks. No need to relive it through a teen replica mini-me.

But there are downsides to being teen-free. Without teens scattered around the house, it's easy to achieve a schleppy look. You might wear a sweater almost as old as you are or adopt a Bellatrix Lestrange hairdo. Or develop a feeling that showers are way over-rated. (Just hypothesizing here.)

Teens give parents a thoughtful heads-up with info, like, "Ugh, dad! You look like you live in an armpit!" Or, "Mom, if you wear that sweater when you're with me I will seriously never speak to you again." (Could that be a temptation to wear the sweater?)

Teens may recommend their favorite influencer to help mold you into shape. They may offer to do your hair which could either be a bonding moment or a trap. Most likely they'll just avoid you in public.

Having younger children around also helps a person face certain truths. Years ago, my nephew, age 6, pointed to a flattering picture of me in my 20's, then pointed to my way-more-than-20 face, and said (rather skeptically for a 6-year-old, I must say), "This doesn't even look like you." Another time, a toddler niece ran to greet me and decisively informed me, jumping with happiness as she spoke, "You are fat!" (In both cases, the parents quickly intervened with comments along the lines of What You Said is Not Ok.)

Conclusion? Some truths are overrated. I'll take lying adults every time. It's true that children do grow up and both the nephew and niece grew into wonderful adults who tell me all the time how attractive I look. I'm sure they're telling the truth.

Yes, I'm Still Sure

Throughout my life, people have checked in on my no-kid decision. In my 40's, my friend introduced her new bundle of joy to me. Her mom was there and looked at me with that hazy, blissful look grandma's get and asked, "Sweetie, don't you want one of your own?" I checked in with my feelings which were, "Crap. How can I answer this and not be rude?" There was no way, so I muttered, "No. Not really." Later, when I was north of five decades, that same beloved person asked, "It's not too late for you, is it?"

2. CONCEPTION IS STILL A THING

It takes a long time for The Question to stop. And then the comments switch gears.

I met a young woman sitting at a party with a baby in her arms who started our conversation by asking (and this is totally true) "How many children do you have?" When I smiled, made the zero sign with my hand, and said "Zilch," she put her hand on my arm and said, "That is so sad." I swear she had tears in her eyes. "I'm...ok," I said, but she sadly shook her head. In her mind, I am living a tragedy. I can live with that.

Most parents consider the bond with their child stronger than Superman. As a childfree gal, would I fight a never-ending battle for the happiness, ease, and safety of another? I believe I feel similar Superperson urges for some of the people I love who I may or may not share genes with. For some, I would leap a tall building. (Though not in a single bound. I am over 60, after all. I'd like, walk up all the stairs and down again.) I acknowledge that the parent/child relationship is something I'll never understand for sure. But when it comes to a strong emotional bond with someone who frequently pisses you off, I get it.

MARVELOUS QUOTE #9

"When the last tiddlywinker had
finally left home for college,
I exhaled for the first time in
decades and said to myself
(I was talking a lot to myself
by then): 'That is that.'
Somehow, I had overlooked the possibility
of our kids' eventually having
kids of their own."

— Maynard Good Stoddard, from "The Wrong
Stuff" in *The Saturday Evening Post*

Your Kids May Have Kids

Some grandparents tell me parenting was meh, but grandparenting is sweet. Maybe the sweetness is the relief of being with someone with zero political opinions. Maybe it's because children will dance in a very silly manner with you. Maybe it's because the little ones get such joy from people they can outrun. Maybe it's the old truism that a grandparent can be endlessly attentive since, ultimately, they get to send the kid home.

Give Us a Break

The birthrate is down, with murmurs of "Yeah, I don't think so" reverberating worldwide when it comes to reproduction. A guest on Stephen Colbert's show said, "Everyone likes babies, right?" Audience members shouted "NO!" and Colbert said, "I don't think everyone agrees."

A flaccid birthrate is good news for those who find children less appealing than toe fungus. But it's a bummer when people make the childfree decision because they realize that earning a living while raising a child seems as likely as Batman and The Joker getting together for a sangria.

The work world is still only slowly embracing no-brainer stuff, like supplying ample time off for working parents to adjust to the new arrival, now forever at the party, who's eating all the guacamole. I hope we've moved on from asking whether parents or childfree people should get equal amounts of work flexibility to the understanding that a norm of rigid work hours is a bad idea for everyone. Even The Joker likes a happy hour Aperol. Flexibility lets everyone enjoy an energizing brew of lifeywork/workylife.

Since a child born now may be my podiatrist down the road (or a designer of comfortable, yet chic, footwear), it seems foolish to oppose robust parental benefits. I want a future podiatrist who has parents with enough time flexibility to bring them to a Foot Museum (yes, there are Foot Museums) and read them many funny stories about feet. I want those parents to have enough stress relief to allow my doc to develop a lovely footside manner. Sensible work benefits improve our world. And feetsies.

Conception is Still a Thing

Do I think people who want kids are insane and deluded? No. Not after knowing parents who considered the choice, felt the desire, and mostly handled both the magnificent and miserable parenting times with grace, patience, and just a few shrieking meltdowns.

A friend was venting to me and reeled off a litany of hair-raising stressors related to her kid. She ended with, "Well, with all that said, I'm really glad she's my daughter." You go, mama. I'm glad she's your daughter, too.

3. OVER-60, CHILD-FREE, & STILL OK?

> **MARVELOUS QUOTE #10**
>
> "All God's children are not beautiful. Most of God's children are, in fact, barely presentable."
>
> — Fran Lebowitz, from her book *Metropolitan Life*

My Cuteness Epiphany

"People who don't love dogs have a hole in their heart." A dog lover told me this after she learned I preferred cats over dogs. Since this person is otherwise callous and bitchy, her comment didn't mean much. Though I

3. OVER-60, CHILDFREE, & STILL OK?

understand the sentiment. As a cat lover, it saddens me when people can't see the appeal in artistically pawed cat litter, a lap in constant use, or a wintry night in bed warmed by a cat hat (an adorable kitty-witty curled around your head!) Overall, if you don't find cats and dogs captivating, even when they're puppies or kittens, the world gives you a pass and your social standing is Ok. This is not true when it comes to itty bitty people.

People have pointed to babies countless times in my life and asked, "Aren't they adorable?" while I remained silent. But recently, I noticed something strange. The first time it happened, I gasped. I felt confused. I chalked it up to a one-time glitch. Then it happened again: I saw a small child and thought, "Oh, how cute." *I even felt a warm little glow when I looked at them.* OK. Odd reaction number two. Excess hormones used to screw with my head, so maybe minimal hormones do the same? Then it happened *again*. While I sat on my porch, bothering no one, a mom pushing her baby in a stroller trundled by and I thought, "How frigging precious is that kid?" As I write this, I'm remembering my horror at the thought. I ran inside to ponder.

Here's my conclusion. My body and brain know there is zero chance I'll get pregnant. They also know there's been no pressure to open our legs specifically for procreation for some time now. Also, why wouldn't babies be cute since miniature things tend to be cute, including baby piggies, newborn chicks, and precious, tiny, dollhouse toilet paper rolls. (Yes, absolutely a thing.) So, I am finally free to react with joy, no strings attached, to a tiny human who is objectively cute, and even cuter since they need supervision. Sort of like my high school boyfriends. Or maybe all my boyfriends. (Not you, old boyfriend reading this. Other old boyfriends.)

This new outlook on baby adorability has changed my life. Though I never wanted children cluttering up the house, *I now see they can be cute!* This is a glorious new phase for me. So many social media posts are now less annoying. When I see a baby, there's a possibility I'll approach it, rather than endanger myself and others by walking backward. I might watch an entire movie with a child other than Chucky as the lead. The possibilities are breathtaking, and I'm glad I've made it to this point.

My brother David grew to be a handsome fellow but at the time of his premature birth he was the ugliest infant on earth. With wrinkled skin not yet fitting his body, he looked more like Yoda than my little bro. As mentioned, throughout my life, I didn't find infants cute,

3. OVER-60, CHILDFREE, & STILL OK?

even though they were all cuter than baby David. But I would never, in a kajillion kazillion years, have shared my feelings. Better my tongue be used to test electrical sockets. THAT's how taboo it is to find infants anything other than bewitchingly cute. Some societal norms are worth challenging, but this is not one of them. All babies are cute; full stop.

Though I now find babies cute to look at, mine is a hands-off admiration. Honestly, I do not need to hold your child. I'm good. At least I no longer dwell so much on infant head size (Big!) and I see the charm in little baby faces, little baby feet, and little baby stares. Though I still wonder, when I tickle their little baby toes, if I will like the big old farting adult they will become.

I still see some adults purse their lips in distaste when a wee one comes by. Friend, you have my support. I may now find some children cute, but I also find you extremely cute. Kids are just one cute thing in a sea of kittens, puppies, and boy bands.

I'll clarify that I don't find all children cute. The cut-off is around nine and they start looking adorable again around the age of BTS boys. I confirmed this feeling when an errand brought me to a local junior high at lunchtime. I walked into the school to what felt like the bowels of Hell. There were *children*, crowded in the front lobby, laughing, running, pushing, congregating, and whispering. They walked aimlessly as if they had nowhere to go. I know they're kids, but is that an excuse for bouncing around like lunatic Pac-Men?

Not one of those youngsters seemed especially cute to me. I can't even fathom what I looked like to them.

I finished my errand and tried to leave. Kids streamed in and out of what seemed like increasingly distant front doors, each child looking at me with no expression in answer to my obvious need to pass them. I matched their non-expressions since I was just looking to survive at that point.

I finally elbowed my way out to the blessedly fresh air where I saw a rumpled young girl sitting alone on the front steps, looking grim. Had she just been teased on social media? Or was she thinking about what fucking losers all the other kids were and imagining her future life as an adult? Walking away from the din to the quiet street was a reminder that I am indeed Ok without a daily dose of cute children.

The Young'uns Have Their Charms

I was lounging with my laptop on a bench-like stone at Denver's lovely Botanic Gardens, tapping in hilarious insights about being childfree, when a serious 4-year-old holding an iced cream approached. (I'm guessing her age; she could have had work and been 6.) She carefully sat next to me. She had a concerned look and stared deep into my eyes. Was she thinking, "Poor lonely lady. Do you need company?" Or maybe, "If this asshole wasn't plopped in the middle of this rock, my entire family could sit here." I'll never know. I chatted cordially with her, asking how she liked the garden and her ice cream, but she just kept licking and staring. It was kind of fascinating since it was so unlike what a sane adult would do. Eventually, the mom walked over and led the child away saying, "They're very attracted to people relaxing on their own."

Overall, children have been good to me. I've never had a child put me in a corner for being bad. No child has made me eat all my veggies or asked if I got a good performance review at work. They are Ok with piercings and tattoos and don't ask me to wear a higher neckline. They don't moderate my online searching, or question whether my social media friend is truly the age they claim (65). They improve my vocabulary by teaching me groovy new words, and it doesn't bother me when they laugh when I say groovy.

I find myself defending the blue-sky ideas of young people and feel a swell of completely unearned pride when one of them does something creative, kind, or brilliant. I haven't contributed my genes to the future mess of humankind, but I can still want the best for it.

MARVELOUS QUOTE #11

"There are moments where you
will have to be a grown-up.
Those moments are tricks.
Do not fall for them."

— Jenny Lawson, from her book *Furiously Happy*

No Kids, No Problems?

Having a child seemed like a nifty possibility for a few months in my life. I had a nice partner, and other couples seemed to pretty much like their children. I was already at the age when my peers' children crept off to god knows where to do god knows what, so the clock was ticking. My sister-in-law advised, "Well if you want to do it, do it soon. Like tomorrow." But I didn't.

When I imagine the road not taken, I don't see the blissful scenarios I missed. I see a life that would have been Ok, but no more Ok than the life I have.

In my childfree readings, I see the phrase "the smug childfree." This refers to those who lord their superior no-kids choice over others. Of course, being childfree doesn't lead to a splendorous life. The truth is, no matter your choices, life, at its best, is quite Ok. Sure, sometimes it's wowie zowie, and sometimes it's just eww. But generally, it's pretty Ok. You can move the needle one way or the other with life choices. My wow needle pings all the time over little wonderful things, and my eww meter regularly hits eleven in a world with low empathy, chicken fingers, and the Gucci Diana Crocodile Tote Bag costing $42,000. I don't feel smug.

Like any group, the childfree-by-choice contingent is not monolithic. Some adore children and have jobs like running tot circuses that pop toddlers from little

3. OVER-60, CHILDFREE, & STILL OK?

cannons. Others aren't crazy about the wee ones and think communities that bar children are wonderful.

Like procreation, no-creation has challenges. For example, if you're childfree, there's no guarantee you'll:

> **Have more time to do anything**. Wasting time is too much fun.
> **Never pee a tiny bit in your pants when laughing.** Mothers claim this happens because they had babies. From the perspective of my pants, this is not true.
> **Ever be free from people asking about your childfree decision.**

What brings joy to life? I'd say it comes through attitude, perception, planning, choices, luck, and, most importantly, comfortable shoes. Also, don't stack the deck against yourself. If pink-painted houses make you queasy; do not paint your house pink. If reading Shakespeare induces a coma; choose Not to Be a Shakespeare reader. If you lean against having children, consider tumbling in that direction. It will not guarantee a splendid existence but you won't pay for an added phone line.

Am I happy childfree? I'd say my days are a mix of crazy happy, pretty happy, meh, disgruntled, and miserable. Things that make me unhappy include:

- Dust.
- My low wine tolerance.
- Being told to be on time for no good reason.
- Yoga.
- Yoga taught by your awesome Yoga teacher.
- Eating apple pie.
- Eating your mom's wildly delicious apple pie.
- Bad acting in a professional theatre.
- No pricing on yard sale items. (Come on people.)
- Revolting politicians.
- Downton Abbey (I can't explain it.)
- Jane Austen novels (Ok. Detecting a pattern here.)
- Continually losing and finding 15 lbs.
- People with zero moral compass (See Revolting politicians, above.)
- My inability to remember names.
- My inability to remember most things.
- My, uh. Something. Never mind.

No one is 100% happy. Maybe your dog. Not my cat. I aim to achieve a median of over 60% happy and given that goal, I feel successful.

3. OVER-60, CHILDFREE, & STILL OK?

There's some evidence I'm more happy than not. There are no sleeping pills in the house to help me slumber through either the night or forever. TikTok videos seem hilarious and not a view into a meaningless void. I Get by With a Little Help From my Friends and, after all these years, I still think Jumping Jack Flash is a gas gas gas.

So many things make me happy. Or maybe content is the word. It must seem phony when I say I'm amazed at things like the variation in a stone façade or the unexplainable satisfaction only oatmeal can bring. As my Maine friend Cheryl says, "Enjoying little things makes us happier people." (Her ability to smile through Maine winters verifies this.)

Just as we can count on adolescents rarely making wise decisions, we can also be sure no one's life is trouble-free. In my life, I've dealt with lethargy, romantic indecision, and figuring out how in the world anyone can make an engineer laugh. All tough things, but none related to making babies. As my wise friend Curt, in Michigan, says, "We're not puppies. We're not happy all the time." (And living through Michigan winters proves his point.) The "who's happier, those with or without children?" question seems one without an answer. Pretty sure, though, that I'm happier when winter is over.

Annoying Assumptions

A few things bug me that are related to being childfree. One is news stories that refer to people in the story by such terms as grandma, mom, dad, and grandpa, even when the story has nothing to do with offspring. Like the headline, *Grandmother Ticketed Driving 115 mph!* Defining a person by whether or not they once used contraception doesn't reveal much. When I read those labels, I look for a connection to a grandkid/kid in the story but am often disappointed. In the speeding story, were the grandkids chasing grandma in their car because she missed her 4 p.m. pill? Were they in grandma's car, clutching the dash-board?

Though family labels are not strong personal descriptors, they do evoke an image for each person to work with. If your grandma is a bargain hunter, the speeding grandma story might make you think, "I bet Grammy was rushing to Walmart!" If your grandma is a chain-smoking creep you might think, "I bet grandma pissed somebody off *again*."

Reporters don't use other random family labels in their stories. Like these.

3. OVER-60, CHILDFREE, & STILL OK?

> "Today an intrepid sister rescued an eagle from an over-zealous cat."
> "That cat was really ambitious," commented a neighborhood daughter."
> "I think the cat deserved to keep the bird," said a local cousin.

Labeling a person based on their relation to birthing does, in fact, say something about the person's life experience. They've all felt, or maybe watched, the enormous effort required to birth a baby. Otherwise, all bets are off. Procreation-centric labels may not help the reader, "said an irritated auntie."

Another sore point for me is that every Mother's Day, without fail, while I'm out minding my own business, a few men I don't know (it's always men), tell me "Happy Mother's Day!" Since it feels to me that it's just as likely the guy is a mom as I am, I want to wish him the same, but I just say thanks. Sometimes saying "thanks" just keeps life moving. I'm curious about the assumption that if a person has a uterus, they've used it. Or that the uterus owner would see it as a compliment if others assume it's been used. It feels presumptuous. Should I congratulate men on their great penis use the night before, since, as penis owners, they surely aim to use them well?

I don't think I need to mention context. A simple, "Great job with your penis" should please most penis owners. I understand it might also confuse them. Which is how I feel when I'm wished a Happy Mother's Day.

My Friends Kids

Since I made the childfree choice, some of my parent pals assume I don't much care about their children. But I do. They're people, and what people do often interests me. I'm easy to please. So, hey, parent pals! I am, in fact, interested in how you and your kid made curtains. I'm psyched that your child won a hip-hop contest (county-wide!) and bummed that they didn't get the lead in Hamilton (Yes, of course, your daughter would have been a better Hamilton than that Ryan kid!) But hearing about your child to the exclusion of anything else makes me wonder if you're otherwise running a meth lab and can't talk about it. In a similar vein, if I get a holiday card with only your children pictured, I think WHERE ARE YOU, PARENTS? I WANT TO SEE YOU! I like seeing the minis, but I know the maxis better.

3. OVER-60, CHILDFREE, & STILL OK?

Some parent pals also assume I'm secretly sad about not having children and I must crave pseudo-parenting or grandparenting time. After all, why else would I give a shit about you and your kid making curtains? I just do. And when it comes to wanting to spend time with kids, just sometimes is good.

A friend told me, "I don't like children, but I like my children." This must be like, "Your fart smells bad, but mine doesn't." Since I don't have any children to like, do I dislike all the children? No. Not all of them. Can running around a park with a child be exhilarating fun? Yes. Can a conversation with a six-year-old be strangely riveting? It's happened more than once. Will I watch your child for a few hours? Depending on the details, my reply could be a hard no, or, if you have a pool and it's warm, a definite yes. Note the keywords here are depending, details, pool, and warm. I may really like your children, but babysitting is a whole other thing.

If you're a parent looking for a free sitter, throw out hints to the potential kid minder and see if they bite. Things like, "Little Agatha loves to see you so much!" Or "My partner and I are going to literally commit hari-kari if we don't get a break from little Agatha." No reaction will tell you a lot. The hari-kari comment would get me to babysit. I'm not heartless and I'd be super impressed by the drama.

Here's a confession to parents of children placed in the care of my young and clueless hands, endless decades ago.

> *I was the most excruciatingly boring young babysitter in history. I allowed your children to watch anything on TV.*
>
> *I once tried to play outdoors with my little charges and it resulted in your thoroughly rotten children hiding in the nearby woods, silently, for hours.*
>
> *I sat in shock when you handed me an actual infant and left.*
>
> *I used quiet time to read my first dirty book which I got from your shelf. (Myra Breckenridge. I had to use a dictionary to look up the word dildo. And it still didn't make sense until years later.)*
>
> *I ate the food in your fridge and almost threw up when I tasted your halvah.*

3. OVER-60, CHILDFREE, & STILL OK?

All the children I babysat wanted my brilliant, creative friend Kathleen to be their babysitter. Kathleen would arrive holding paints, clay, and brightly colored cloth scraps to create kingdoms. She stood ready to shower the young ones with wisecracking humor, warmth, imagination, and love. Their youthful bitterness was deep when I walked in the door holding nothing but an expression of ill-concealed panic. This may explain their quiet hours in the woods. I was pretty sure they were plotting something that would hurt. What hurt most was when the parents came home and paid me a fifth of typical babysitter pay. (Kathleen told me these awful parents did this to her as well. Don't do this, parents!)

I sometimes did well with children I babysat. I think these kids sensed that they needed to lead the way. Oh, yes, and they weren't spoiled little bastards like the forest kids. I'm quite good at following a child's lead, and over the years I've even come to understand when I should definitely not be following their lead. We keep learning. For me, after watching children for a couple of hours, I don't mull over missed life opportunities. I think about how childcare workers deserve much more pay.

Some childfree-by-choice folks enjoy tiny humans, and some detest them. The latter don't want to bop kids on the noggin, they just don't want to hang with them. Since math can help with understanding, here are some informative percentages:

- Some people stink at communicating with children **100%** of the time.
- There are adults whose goal is to spend **0%** of their time with children.
- **25%** of all adults have moments where they dream there are no children on earth and instead people are born fully grown with the knowledge and moral development level of adults.
- **On any controversial topic,** about **45%** passionately agree; **44%** angrily disagree, and **11%** say "Wha?"

- I made up **100%** of those statistics.

And now, a data-driven look at the life of one intentionally childfree person:

- **Times I'm depressed or lonely**: A lot.
- **Times I think life isn't worth the effort**: A few.
- **Times the wretched feelings above come from being childfree**: None.
- **Times I feel joy and well-being**: A lot.
- **Times that feelings of joy and well-being come from being childfree**: Some.
- **Times I enjoy babysitting**: It's happened.
- **Times I want to take children home after babysitting**: It has not happened.
- **Clueless remarks I make to parents about parenting, since I don't get their situation**: I've lost count.

Tiny But Tidy

I read a news piece that said, "The more subversive the children's book, the better." It said books about butts, farts, and making a mess delight all children. I beg to differ.

As a child, I enjoyed the book *Cat in the Hat*. The verses and illustrations are great, but as the Cat slowly wrecked the house while the parents were away, I could feel my tiny little self hyperventilating. The high-pitched little girl scream in my head said, "I do not like a mess, Mr. Stupid Cat in the Stupid Hat!"

Though age has made me messier (Is there any real reason to make a bed?) throughout life I've been a neatener. So, keep in mind, if you give birth, you could have an incredibly fun kid who finds filth hilarious. Or, you could have me. (And if you already are me, good luck with that kid.)

I'm a compulsive tidier. The kind of person who sits on different places on the sofa each time so as not to wear out just one spot. Being like this annoys visiting parents who say, "Shit! Even the towels in your closet are neat!" I've screwed up when I've said to parents, "Well, I don't have kids," which sounds like I'm insinuating their house looks like crap. A stupid thing for me to say, really, since untidy-home guilt is a total waste of guilt.

I've learned that a shiny clean home is not on the important-things-in-life list. When I visit people the things I notice are groovy knick-knacks, comfy chairs, and whether or not there are snacks. (There should be snacks.)

Sure, a minor cleaning effort is appreciated when I visit others. Some houses have invisible floors since you can't see them through the knee-deep stuff that falls on the floor and that anyone else in their freaking right mind would pick up. Even piles are fine if a reasonable path is created, sharp edges are dulled, and nothing is moving. Overall, I'd rather get some good snacks.

The Parents Gang

Parents who are reading this (all are welcome here!) know they get to be in the Parents Club. They have a membership whether they want it or not. Once you claim a child as your own, the tentacles of Other Parents slither your way. The Other Parents offer solace, understanding, and support. They share honest and rueful laughter over the antics of the little ones. They suggest you guys trade off on babysitting. They offer child-rearing advice you didn't ask for. They freely and frequently comment on your ridiculous and pathetic parenting skills.

We childfree folks don't have a club. Sure, there are childfree groups and venting outlets, but you have to actively join in order to kvetch. In my experience, when childfree people meet, we may share an information-free sentence about our choice, like "Yeah, I never wanted kids." Or "My sister had the kids in my family." Or "I hate the goddamn little shits."

It could be argued that parents get a life-long sense of belonging because parents share their children's triumphs and foibles with each other. But parents also share those with anyone who will listen, so I can be in the gang, too! I can't share personal tales of childbirth, but just as rock stars need an audience, so do parents. As an enthralled listener, I've got the best seats in the house when it comes to hair-raising childbirth stories. Almost like being there! Only I'm dancing and waving around my lighter and not actually birthing a child. Best. Seats. In the House.

3. OVER-60, CHILDFREE, & STILL OK?

MARVELOUS QUOTE #12

"Have you ever listened to people with kids talk to other people with kids? It is a strange and confusing language that I don't ever want to understand. I don't ever want to listen to two people debating over whether school lunches should be non-GMO. I have absolutely zero opinions on things like that. Also, I would buy my kid a hundred TVs just to get him right on up out of my goddamn face."

—Samantha Irby, from her book *we are never meeting in real life*

Still Crazy After All These Years?

Have you seen the mini-series *Click Bait*? If not, there's a major spoiler coming in a few words. I enjoyed the twisty turns in the show until they revealed the culprit. The perp was a bored childfree woman with nothing better to do than impersonate a man online and stalk insecure women. This led to the murder of the innocent, impersonated man. When we meet the stalker woman early on, she says she has no children but, "It's totally fine! My husband and I keep busy!" Later she explains it was boredom that prompted her insane actions.

Here's some advice. If you decide to stroll the childfree path, do not fill your time by impersonating anyone online. In case it needs to be said, also do not put together a heist gang and try to nab a well-guarded historic treasure. Likewise, don't rob your neighbors' homes, make prank phone calls, or push down old people and run away. Instead, search "Bored?" online. You'll find meetup groups like the Jane Austen Book Club, The Chicken Enthusiasts, the Gathering of the Different, and The Church That Used to Meet in the Pub. All real groups. As well as four billion other things you might consider doing, childfree or not, to keep you occupied and out of prison.

3. OVER-60, CHILDFREE, & STILL OK?

Who Loves Ya, Baby?

A friend told me she sometimes feels her childfree choice diminishes her value to society. She feels compelled to over-achieve to prove she's using her non-child time in a productive way. I was surprised and disturbed to hear my esteemed friend say this! Just what defines a valuable life? Take mine, for example.

I make a delectable matzoh ball soup, I enjoy helping people move to a new home (really!), and the slight smile I achieve in some pictures is perfect. So, despite having a lonely womb, I earn my keep.

Aside from the obvious value of people who are healthcare workers, firefighters, fast cashiers, or sober zipline operators, there's value in so many things people do.

We can value the co-worker who brings pleasure to a job that's less joyful than a used tissue.

We can value the effort needed to keep friends. Like that friend who has never been on time. Never.

We can value those who help others when the need is real, while keeping their radar on for potential soul-sucking scumbags.

We can value those who create simple, extravagant, or bizarre beauty through art or their everyday choices. The friend who is never on time is best at all of this, of course.

We can value those who listen to our bitching and take away our thoughts of wanting to strangle someone.

We can value someone who makes a day survivable by sharing something funny or remarkable. (Did you know an avocado never ripens on a tree? No shit!)

We can value those who make us smile despite ourselves when they dress as caped crusaders, starship officers, sexy warriors, or very furry creatures. Though no button eyes, please.

We can value the person who's not burned out on childcare, since they don't have a child, so they can watch a child, even once. (Parents will remember this one time and elevate the act for years. Thank you, parents.)

3. OVER-60, CHILDFREE, & STILL OK?

We can value educators since something we learn may help us MacGyver our way out of entrapment by a fourth-dimensional warlord.

The point is that caring for a child is just one valuable thing in a universe of warlords waiting to pounce. To my friend who questions her value, I say: You've got this.

Things You Can Do With Pets, Not Kids #4

Use money on continuing education for yourself, not them.

College Cat-alog
- Cute Body Poses 101: Guaranteed "Aww" Getters
- Waking Up Your Human: Beyond the Loud Meow
- Moving Items With No Thumbs Both Gently and With Destructive Intent
- Quick Food Rejection: Not Even a Bite

No Perfect Choice

As mentioned earlier, no matter your choices, likes, or dislikes in life, people will be there to tell you what a fucking idiot you are. Labeling others as stupid is a human pastime. We are endlessly judgmental and judged over both important and trivial stuff. Don't love Adele's music? *Heathen!* Ok with cheap wine? *For god's sake, were you raised in a pig sty?* Voted for a person I did not vote for? *Just die, why don't you?*

As someone whose hair should be gray, I'm judged both on coloring my hair and what color I color my hair (Not pink or purple? Who are you trying to kid with that *brown?*)

I judge people who buy the Gucci Diana Crocodile Tote Bag for $42,000. Wrong on so many levels.

Likewise, choosing to be childfree brings on judgments. *Shallow. Immature. Unloving. Damaged.* You know the phrase "live and let live?" It's a complete lie. Thankfully, choosing to be childfree is not punishable by death. Only by nagging.

Is it stigmatizing to be childfree? Try being old or not really slim. All I can say is *get in line stigmas*. If you choose

3. OVER-60, CHILDFREE, & STILL OK?

childfree, there will always be those who don't believe it's your deliberate choice. Especially if you're older.

Here's stuff people believe about those who are old and childfree.

> **They think**: Cute stories about their children fill you with feelings of sorrow and loss.
> **But the truth is**: Cute kid stories are cute.
> **They think**: You just ran out of time.
> **But the truth is**: You took care to tell potential life partners about your decision to say not to a tot.
> **They think**: Your life is sad.
> **But the truth is**: Your life is Ok.
> **They think**: Your life is an endlessly fun disco dance since you have no responsibility for child-rearing.
> **But the truth is**: Your life is Ok.

The moral is life tends to be Ok and we all can and should enjoy a little disco.

Sure, there are consequences when you choose the childfree curtain. You may win the washer/dryer combo or you may hear the zonk noise and win a pile of Spam. Actual consequences include rarely having eyes rolled at you, never needing to hear the song *Let it Go*, and more pudding for you.

To those who are pulled to parenthood and can't have their wish fulfilled, I empathize. The sadness of your situation is genuine. Still, I hope you'll do what you can to bring beloved kids into your life, even if they're not yours.

It's hard to get all we yearn for. I want to travel everywhere, eliminate world hunger, and cuddle with Scott Bakula, John Baptiste, and Ryan Reynolds. Preferably all at once. Or any BTS boy. (They're all over 18, right?) Turns out I can travel a bit, support hunger relief programs, gaze at Scott, John, and Ryan in a million pictures and videos, and the BTS guys in a trillion. These alternatives aren't as satisfying as the original wish, but they're not bad.

If you love to be with children for their youthful zest, you can find those zesty kids! They are not hiding in sewers or cleverly concealed on a top shelf you can't reach without schlepping out the step ladder. They are *everywhere*. Ok. Don't walk up to children at the park without asking the caregiver. (Sadly, the world can be less like *The Cosby Show* and more like Bill Cosby.) If you offer to babysit, you will instantly find a child's

3. OVER-60, CHILDFREE, & STILL OK?

hand in yours and no sign of the parent. (The parents will return. Eventually.)

The child supply is ample and they want company, need support, and are happy to put a sticky hand on your face. You'll be surprised at how much you can enjoy wee ones who don't have your last name. Co-worker's children. Relative's children. The neighbor you don't know down the block's children. Harried parents will gladly supply you with a loaner. If you don't want the kid to go home for at least 18 years, there are children who'd love to settle in with you. (Through adoption. You can't keep random children.)

Poor Old Childfree Me

I'm not yet ancient, but definitely on the tail end of the boogie. Living a whole lot of decades has supplied perspective, experience, and the knowledge that I'll never have a favorite color since I like so many colors.

The narrative related to the childfree choice changes for older women. You're no longer that cheeky gal who sauntered against the tide. You're the weirdo who couldn't nab a sperm supplier.

This is where my many years of living come in handy since I can swim in my sea of self-confidence and a nicely-matured feeling of not giving a shit about what others think. (Mostly.)

When I had a career, I'd sometimes work a 14-hour day on a project that didn't cure cancer but had meaning in my groovy little cosmos. "Tsk, tsk," friends told me. "Stop working so hard. Your job won't love you back when you leave." True, and after I left, my job also never asked me for a loan, a place to live, or funding for a wedding. The flow and fulfillment of those work times were building blocks for living now. Though I now avoid 14-hour work days.

It's true that work never calls to wish me a happy birthday or share a random phone call. They say something about being busy.

Parents Are Never Lonely #3

Hi There! I can't answer right now! or ever! LOL! PM Me!

Hello? Sweetie? Hello?

You're Welcome

Oh, dear children I never had. I imagine the many ways you would have felt damaged if I'd raised you.

- By taking you to Goodwill rather than anywhere with new clothes.
- By letting you watch online programs unsupervised, and then wondering how you knew the phrase "suction therapy."
- By refusing to finance an expensive wedding since potlucks are hilarious fun and why not?
- By playing way too much Beatles music.
- By teaching you schedules are just a suggestion.

My darling non-existent children, I would have inflicted mental scars on you by

- Buying you a second-hand car instead of the designer handbag you wanted (that was the same price as the Chevy.)
- Insisting that chickens absolutely do not have fingers.
- Confusing you through advocating both spontaneity and planning.
- Correcting your grammar.

3. OVER-60, CHILDFREE, & STILL OK?

- Encouraging second and third helpings at meals.
- Telling you the definition of "conspicuous consumption" and stressing it was not a good thing.
- Allowing you to make so many of your own childhood decisions, you would not have survived to adulthood.

The nail in your poor upbringing coffin would have been hammered when I assured you that singing John Denver's *Thank God, I'm a Country Boy* in public would not harm your popularity. Though you would have been smart enough to ignore me on that one.

As an aunt, I can share all those things in dribs and drabs, no harm done, and you are free to roll your eyes.

There are things I'll never experience in my childfree existence. Though I will never need to make a pumpkin Halloween costume (a positive), I will also never experience an inedible but touching Mother/Father's Day breakfast in bed (probably a negative.) Though I don't need to learn the lyrics to *Let It Go* (a positive), I may not be alerted to great new music (a bummer for sure. Though maybe I can ask my BTS friends.) Though I can avoid paying for a child's wedding (a positive), I sometimes feel inclined to contribute a small amount to every child on earth, since I have no child-raising expenses. I can only say that the cost of every child on earth adds up.

MARVELOUS QUOTE #13

"I enjoy kids, but not for long periods. I think they're adorable and funny and sweet, and then I have a headache."

—**Kim Cattrall, from an interview in *The Advocate***

We learn so much on our life path and build treasured memories. A mom and dad learn not to open a boy's diaper too quickly, and will always remember their child's first zombie-like steps. In my work in a college library, I learned not everyone working for a university is the least bit bright, and recall the almost visible lightbulb-over-the-head moments when a student realized I told them something that wasn't stupid and maybe helpful.

I used to think the passage of time would be less obvious without kids at home phasing from bassinet to basement. Not true. Wrinkle-free celebrities in their

3. OVER-60, CHILDFREE, & STILL OK?

90's may briefly make us believe that time stands still, but in reality, it speeds ahead. I know this when I look in the mirror and see a puzzled old gal gazing back at me. I know this because my friends have embraced Help-I've-fallen-and-I-can't-get-up technology. I know time marches along when I see my friends with their - it's still hard to say it - *grandchildren*.

For those who are certain I've screwed up by not prioritizing procreation, I can only say oh well and ding dang. Here we are. I know myself. I've briefly envied those in jobs I didn't choose, including lead singer in a jazz ensemble, ice cream truck driver, and Gypsy Rose Lee-style stripper. In a similar vein, there have been seconds in my life when I wondered if one of my names should have been Mom. I went for the stroll instead of the stroller.

Before I close, let me bust some childfree myths. If you don't love cats, don't panic. Being childfree will not fill your house with cats. Or dogs. Or make you vote in any particular way. Even the smartest way. Or make you enjoy craft projects more than you do now. With or without children you will, as the young'uns say, do you.

If parenthood is your passionate goal, I say hurrah for you! If you're my pal and remember me after the birth, I'll still be there for you. Sometimes.

And me? I'm Ok.

BOOK CLUB QUESTIONS

1. Were there comments in the book that particularly resonated with you?

2. Do you have any thoughts on why the author chose "Ok" in the title instead of a word like "Terrific!"?

3. The author doesn't touch much on the population ramifications of having children. Is this a problematic omission?

4. What were your least favorite ideas in the book?

5. What were your favorite ideas in the book?

6. Do you know how amazing you are to be discussing ideas?

ACKNOWLEDGMENTS

Thank you to those who helped me refine the book title. Early contenders were *No Kids, Bloody Old, and Still Ok* and *Womb with a View: Childfree Life from Over the Hill* (the latter was a favorite of mine that was roundly hated by all.) Thank you for the comments from Orlando Archibeque, Annie Benedetto, Jenny Henke, Karen Sobel, and Liz Willis. Title suggestions included:

> Holly Bean's *I'm Okay, You're Not Okay Because You Have Done Everything to Make Your Kid Have a Wonderful Life Only to be Stripped of Your Pride, Your Wealth, and Your Youth, Then Abandoned and Crushed Like a Dried Out, Empty Husk*
>
> Lorrie Evans' *Just Not Kids*
>
> Marical Farner's *Hot Flashes Not Diaper Rashes*

Alana Lykin's *Life Beyond the Womb - Still A Rewarding Adventure*

Susan Norton's *Still Gleefully Child Free at 63!*

Hazel Robinson's *Retired with No Children*

Marcela and Paul Solari's *No Kids, No Problems*

And Liz D'Antonio Gan, who came up with the final book title!

Thank you to Rich Metter who recovered my deeply deleted manuscript document. You saved me weeks of rewriting. Thanks, also, for the emotional support and practical input, always. Your hilarious writing inspires me though I manage to be only half as good a writer as you.

Mark Brissenden, thank you for correcting my manuscript errors and for being an utterly splendid person in my life.

Sommer Browning, you amazing poet, comedian, editor, mother, human, and author of *Bad Actors*, thank you for doing the first read on the manuscript. You taught me that schtupping is funny, but schtupping in an abandoned warehouse is funnier.

Thank you, April Allridge, for yet again reading a manuscript and for your decades of mentoring and friendship.

Many thanks to Cara Jean Reimann for the help with the cartoon alt text.

Loving thank you's to Cynthia Hashert, Chris Woods, Woody Woods, Val Miller, Gary Hutchison, Mary K. Dodge, Rod Osburn, Elaine Jurries, Peg Christon, Gayle Bradbeer, and Davette Zinik for your ideas and words of support.

To my beloved nieces and nephews, by both blood and choice, please forgive me.

And my thanks to Laura Goodman, a sister-of-the-heart and a talented artist. Laura, I hope you won't be too badly shocked by my stick figure cartoons.

Ellen Metter tried out a number of professions, including radio DJing, dishwashing, mystery shopping, and stand-up comedy. She spent three decades as an academic librarian on Denver's Auraria campus and is the author of the sci-fi novel *Transference*. She enjoys walking anywhere and singing along.